Lover, Unwrap Me

A COLLECTION OF SENSUAL POETRY

Jerilee Anderson

BALBOA.
PRESS
A DIVISION OF HAY HOUSE

Balboa Press books may be ordered through booksellers or by contacting:

Balboa Press
A Division of Hay House
1663 Liberty Drive
Bloomington, IN 47403
www.balboapress.com
1-(877) 407-4847

Because of the dynamic nature of the Internet, any web addresses or
links contained in this book may have changed since publication and
may no longer be valid. The views expressed in this work are solely those
of the author and do not necessarily reflect the views of the publisher,
and the publisher hereby disclaims any responsibility for them.

The author of this book does not dispense medical advice or prescribe
the use of any technique as a form of treatment for physical, emotional,
or medical problems without the advice of a physician, either directly
or indirectly. The intent of the author is only to offer information
of a general nature to help you in your quest for emotional and
spiritual well-being. In the event you use any of the information in
this book for yourself, which is your constitutional right, the author
and the publisher assume no responsibility for your actions.

Any people depicted in stock imagery provided by Thinkstock are
models, and such images are being used for illustrative purposes only.
Certain stock imagery © Thinkstock.

Printed in the United States of America.

ISBN: 978-1-4525-7846-0 (sc)
ISBN: 978-1-4525-7847-7 (e)

Balboa Press rev. date: 8/16/2013

Thank you!

Heartfelt thanks and love to my husband,
John .

For a lifetime of their
support, encouragement
and especially their unconditional Love,
thanks to my parents:
Jim & Lois Anderson
who loved each other for over sixty years
"For (much more than) Sentimental Reasons."

Special thanks to my dear friend,
Vinnie,
who was the first to read these poems
and when I told him I needed a
picture to go with each poem, he said
"You don't need pictures.
The words stand alone."
and he was right!

Deepest gratitude and much love
to all of my family & my dear friends.
(You know who you are.)

Without these special people
this book would not exist.

Foreword

Once upon a time, I was alone. Having recently divorced, I desired a nourishing partnership this time. I wanted to share my life with someone special. I wanted us to spiritually "peel" each other's layers and try to discover the depth of our souls. Soul mating.

One night, I lay awake, words roaming through my mind. I couldn't sleep. The words just kept flowing, swirling, nagging. Eventually, the words grouped into poems or pieces of poems. I kept a pad of paper and a pen near my bed to capture them in the night or risk them vanishing by morning like a dream.

The words would tumble out, sometimes in a line or two, sometimes virtually finished in three lines with five, seven and five syllables. Over the period of three to four weeks, I had dozens of them.

"These are good", I thought. "Could they be my words? Where did they come from?" It wasn't forced. They just kept coming. I wanted to share them, but wasn't sure how to go about it. I arranged them in order (they seemed to have a natural progression).

Some are exactly as they came to me, some new ones have been added. Now this collection is available to everyone. I am happy. I share my life, my heart, my soul, and my future and encourage you to do the same. Keep "peeling"!

With much Love, Jerilee

For Lovers

"*The hours I spend with you I look upon as sort of a perfumed garden, a dim twilight, and a fountain singing to it. You and you alone make me feel that I am alive. Other men it is said have seen angels, but I have seen thee and thou art enough.*"
- **George Moore**

"*I almost wish we were butterflies and liv'd but three summer days - three such days with you I could fill with more delight than fifty common years could ever contain.*"
- **John Keats**

"*Grow old along with me! The best is yet to be.*"
- **Robert Browning**

"*My bounty is as boundless as the sea, my love as deep; the more I give to thee, The more I have, both are infinite.*"
- **William Shakespeare**

Un-wrap

Transitive verb

Definition of unwrap:

to remove or open the wrapping of,

disclose

as in: unwrap a package

First known use of unwrap: 14th century

Other words for "unwrap": bare, break the seal, bring to light, cast off, clear, deobstruct, develop, disclose, discover, dismask, doff, douse, draw the veil, drop, expose, free, impart, lay bare, lay open, let daylight in, let out, manifest, open, open up, patefy, put off, raise the curtain, remove, reveal, show, show up, slip out of, step out of, strip bare, take off, throw off, unblock, uncase, unclench, uncloak, unclog, unclutch, uncork, uncover, uncurtain, undo, undrape, unfold, unfoul, unfurl, unkennel, unlatch, unlock, unmask, unpack, unplug, unroll, unscreen, unseal, unsheathe, unshroud, unshut, unstop, unveil.

What people are saying about
<u>Lover, Unwrap Me</u>

In this great little book Jerilee expresses her love without inhibition. One refreshing poem after another. One can't help but think she has mastered the art of poetry in a Ruminesque way. This book is here to remind ourselves to express love to the ones we LOVE. Let yourself be unwrapped, loved, and taken away by her beautiful, heartfelt words.
- Anja Middelveld, L.Ac., Healing Path Holistic Medicine Clinic, LLC, Milwaukie, Oregon

"stunningly beautiful, touching, relevant, soulful, emotional, loving, sweet, endearing… gosh I can't say enough about this treasure of a little book!! Love its sweet size. The poems that are so brief yet so touching. I see it as a lovely book one could have on a side table in a living room as well as on a bedside table -- where one could pick it up at any moment and read one or two poems or leaf through it reading many. One could easily enjoy just a whisper of an emotion with one poem or get completely engrossed in it with all its lovely emotions projected in many samplings. And what a lovely gift it will make -- for a lover or for a dear friend! Appealing to so many! **- Kathleen Pozzi, Portland, Oregon**

Lover, unwrap me.

I give the gift of my love.

Share my heart and soul.

Lover, befriend me.

Friendship is love's foundation.

Build ours together.

Lover, feel my gaze.

A butterfly flutters by,

forwardly flirting.

4

Lover, magical!

Our first moments together,

always in my heart.

5

Lover, laugh with me.

Tease me, tickle, surprise me!

Life's more fun with you.

Lover, walk with me.

Feel the sand between our toes,

salt water splashing.

Lover, dance with me.

Spinning in each other's arms,

leading, following.

Lover, romance me.

There's candlelight in your eyes,

sweet wine on your lips.

Lover, sit by me.

Sharing sushi side by side,

sipping sweet sake.

Lover, amuse me.

I take pleasure from your laugh,

joy in your presence.

Lover, amaze me.

Reveal your layers to me.

You fascinate me.

Lover, grow with me.

Rearrange, transform, and change.

Better together.

13

Lover, lie with me.

Feel the sun warming our skin

on the grass so green.

Lover, share the moon.

When we are apart, look up.

See our moon, our stars.

Lover, accept me.

Allow the gift of my love.

I give it freely.

Lover, I trust you.

I share with you my secrets,

my hopes, desires.

Lover, believe me.

Open up your heart to me.

You are safe with me.

Lover, awaken.

Even trees cry out for spring.

Rebirth is at hand.

Lover, untie me.

Let loose the bonds of my past.

Free me to be me.

Lover, unlock me.

You hold the key to my heart.

Our love's the treasure.

21

Lover, celebrate!

It's fate. Thank our lucky stars!

You're my destiny.

22

Lover, New Year's Eve!

Seal next year with a promise,

last year with a kiss.

23

Lover, share with me,

my todays, my tomorrows.

Unwrap life with me.

Lover, touch my life.

Just like ripples in a pond,

I flow back to you.

Lover, color me.

Rainbow's dazzling light within.

Without you, life's gray.

Lover, I'm grateful!

I've waited all of my life

for the love of you.

Lover, "I love you.

For sentimental reasons,

I give you my heart."

Lover, support me.

Hold me in your arms so safe.

Share your strength with me.

29

Lover, hold my hand.

Fingers gently embracing.

My heart catches fire.

Lover, arouse me.

I have been numb for so long,

awaiting your touch.

Lover, make music.

Outside rhythms ebb and flow.

Love's song plays within.

—

Lover, delight me.

My heart and soul join with yours.

Joy flows in my life.

33

Lover, surprise me!

Wild, wacky, wonderful,

something just for me.

34

Lover, treasure us.

Realize what a gift we share

to find love so rare.

Lover, pleasure me.

The glow of love's warming light

is waiting for us.

36

Lover, come, join me.

My heart, body, mind and soul;

all these await you.

37

Lover, our eyes meet,

silently declaring love.

The world falls away.

Lover, in your arms!

For days, hours, weeks, months, years,

I am safely home.

Lover, talk to me.

Your voice so sweet and sexy.

Words I love to hear.

Lover, seduce me.

My senses reel when you're near.

Whisper in my ear.

Lover, enjoy me.

Light a fire, pour some wine.

Cuddle up with me.

Lover, flow with me.

Run your fingers through my hair.

Touch me, linger there.

Lover, purr for me.

Soft strokes against skin so warm.

Love flows through my hands.

44

Lover, invite me.

Wrap yourself all around me.

I'm home in your arms.

Lover, ignite me.

Just one glance and I'm aflame.

Passion burns within.

Lover, light my fire.

Fan my flame and stir my coals.

Warm me to my soul.

Lover, I need you.

You fill my life with meaning.

My soul craves its mate.

Lover, undress me.

My skin hungers for your eyes.

Behold my body.

Lover, caress me.

Touch me tenderly tonight.

My skin aches for you.

Lover, possess me.

I am yours for the taking.

Our love's spell is cast.

51

Lover, unwind me.

My silkworm's cocoon wrapped tight,

gently pull my thread.

Lover, breathe with me.

Yin and yang, swirling, flowing,

energy merging.

Lover, embrace me.

You hold my heart in your hands.

Our bodies are one.

Lover, enhance me.

Feel the chemistry, the heat.

Our souls reunite.

55

Lover, desire me.

Our passion flows, passion grows,

passion shows our love.

Lover, come with me.

Soft, silken sheets await us.

Slip into my bed.

Lover, cover me.

Let me feel your weight, your breath

warm against my skin.

58

Lover, smell of me,

love's fresh and musky fragrance.

Deeply breathe my scent.

Lover, look at me.

My heart surges, then races,

waves of desire.

Lover, taste of me.

Our lips linger, tongues entwined.

Kiss me deep, deeper.

Lover, enfold me.

Wrap, twist and wind around me.

Can't get close enough.

Lover, explore me,

to the depth of my being.

Touch me, adore me.

Lover, merge with me,

above, below, soft and hard,

the tao of our love.

Lover, restore me.

Enter our pleasure garden,

Eden in your arms.

65

Lover, cherish me.

Fall into my waiting arms.

Share the fantasy!

Lover, recharge me.

Silken legs wrap thighs of steel.

Sparks fly, juices flow.

Lover, ecstasy!

It's ours to take, ours to make.

Share your love with me.

68

Lover, move the earth.

Take me to the highest heights.

Share in the tremors.

Lover, sleep with me.

Share my body, share my bed,

from dusk until dawn.

Lover, share our "now".

So caught up in this moment,

no future, no past.

71

Lover, spoon with me.

Wrap me, curve against my back,

Earthly paradise.

Lover, live with me.

Share my life, my heart, my home.

Be with me always.

Lover, give to me,

the gift of your tomorrows.

The future is ours.

Lover, complete me.

Fill our days with each other,

from this day forward.

Lover, comfort me.

Your presence halves my sorrow,

and doubles my joy.

Lover, together.

Live, love, laugh and be happy!

Double happiness!

Lover, unveil me.

My soul lies deeply buried.

For your eyes only.

Lover, age with me.

Let's blend like fine, rich, red wine,

much better with time.

Lover, in my dreams!

Happily ever after,

once upon a time...

Lover, forever!

Eternity lends us time.

Please spend it with me.

About the Author

Jerilee was born, lives and works in Portland, Oregon with her husband, John and the first dog she has ever loved, their Norwegian Elkhound, Val.

Lover, Unwrap Me is her first book. She is currently finishing a new book called Mother, Unwrap Me about the special relationship between a mother and her child/children.

Thank you, dear reader,

for sharing my words, your time.

Remember, enjoy!